My Father Was De-pressed

The Key To "Meant All Health" Recovery

It's A Rap

A lifestyle Choice

By Olivia Johnson

Copyright © 2021 Olivia Johnson

First Edition 2021

ISBN: 9798749888782

I fixed my head

From a father of dread

I fixed my head

To avoid the Dead

He was not there

And hit me too

He was not there

And I could not swear

And so I was always aware

I was always looking

Around

In case he was there

Not making a sound

He isolated me

And made me feel bad

He was meant to be my father

And that made me mad

I was not allowed to talk

I was not allowed to say

what I thought

I was forced to smile at him

And to be polite

It was all such a fright

And not very nice

I served him too

To make him feel good

I dared not scare him

As he would hit me

And then I would not

Be free

So I served his every whim

In case he told me off

As I did not want to be

Like little Jack Frost

Who was just lost

I did not realise

At the time

As kids are resilient

As they show

But I was in fact

As depressed as low

This all came up

When I grew up

Out it came

Out of me

It scared

The hell out of me

As I could not see a

Way out

And it left me with loads

Of Doubt

And the Doctor said

When I was unwell

"Depressed"

I never knew then

What that meant

My father was not there

He made me so sad

He put me in a family

Where there was no family

So there I was

Aged 6, I think

Just living on

The total brink

But I did not have to think

I was on the brink

As I was in the link

And so I would not sink

I fixed my head

With my fathers dread

I fixed my head

To avoid the Dead

He was not there

And hit me too

He was not there

And I did not care

And so I was always

Aware

I was always looking

Around

In case he was there

Not making a sound

In case I was found

He isolated me

And made me feel bad

He was meant to be
My father

And that made me mad

So after decades

Of counselling

And plenty of strife

It was like waking up

Just in the night…

But with a lot of light

When I found out

My fathers fright

And that it had been

All out of sight

I gasped at the truth

And leapt up to tell

I realised now

I could end his spell

It was the

Professional Help

From the Certified kind

That helped me through

This journey of mind

It takes lots of work

It is a Lifestyle choice

Covering many decades

That was my choice

But I would encourage

Anyone

To enter this space

And understand

It is a type of race

About the Author

This is the story of how the author became aware in counselling and obtaining Insight and awareness, that the relationship her father had with her in her childhood had a lot to do with the Mental Health Problems she experienced later on in her life as an adult.

This was revealed to her through very extensive and lengthy counselling, that in her case covered many decades..

Prior to her journey of Mental Health Recovery she had no idea that a person's upbringing as a child, under the primary carers, could have such a negative impact on her mental health as a child leading into an adult.

She feels by highlighting her own experiences people can be aware that a good emotional and mental health upbringing in a child will probably lead to more of a healthier mental health existence for the child, both as a child and also as an adult.

.

The author experienced **emotional neglect in childhood** from a very young age.

She happened to find herself on a continual mental health recovery journey in her early 30's,

Through no fault of her own.

She was **experiencing an empty life**. And then she discovered what was needed was a Lifestyle choice.

The choice to dedicate herself to her own Mental Health Recovery with the help of her friends and family.

Disclaimer

This book is designed to provide information and motivation to its readers.

It is sold with the understanding that neither the publisher nor author are engaged to provide any type of

psychological, legal or any other kind of professional mental health advice.

It is purely an expression of the author's own personal mental health journey and her or his reflections

upon it, and not that of the publisher.

Neither the publisher nor the author shall be liable for any physical, psychological, emotional,

financial or commercial damages including, but not limited to special, incidental, consequential or other damages.

Our views and rights are the same.

The reader is responsible for their own choices, actions and results as a result of reading this book.

Printed by Amazon Italia Logistica S.r.l.
Torrazza Piemonte (TO), Italy

53880036R00016